salmonpoetry

The Place Where I Left You

SANDRA ANN WINTERS

salmonpoetry

Published in 2014 by
Salmon Poetry
Cliffs of Moher, County Clare, Ireland
Website: www.salmonpoetry.com
Email: info@salmonpoetry.com

ISBN 978-1-908836-93-9

COVER ARTWORK: © *Can Stock Photo Inc. / rhphoto*
COVER DESIGN & TYPESETTING: *Siobhán Hutson*
Printed in Ireland by Sprint Print

For

Stephen Arthur Beese

And

Steven Harrell Rentz

Acknowledgments

"Death of Alaska" won the 2011 Gregory O'Donoghue International Poetry Competition sponsored by the Munster Literature Centre in Ireland. The editors of the *North Carolina Literary Review* nominated "Water Signs" for the 2011 Pushcart Prize. A manuscript *Who is that Woman* was a semi-finalist in the 2012 Summer Literary Seminars, Unified Literary Contest sponsored by Concordia University in Montreal, Canada. "Talking to Okra won first place in the 2012 Carteret Writers 21st Annual Writing Contest. "My Kitchen" was a runner-up in the 2012 Randall Jarrell Poetry Competition. "Still Life" received an Honorable Mention in the 2012 Deane Ritch Lomax Poetry Competition. "A Living Will," "The Parlour," and "Talking to Okra" were finalists in the 2011 Press 53 Open Poetry Award. "Aw Go Away Now and Again" was a finalist in the Rita Dove Poetry Award in 2010. "The Deaf Dog" was a finalist in the *Inkwell Journal*'s fourteenth annual poetry contest, 2010, judged by Mark Doty.

Thanks to Finishing Line Press for publishing the chapbook *Calving Under the Moon*.

Acknowledgements are due to the editors of the following publications where some of these poems appeared:
Cork Literary Review, Volume XV: "A Master Could Make Flesh of Marble," "Knocknagullane, Ireland," "A Living Will," "Talking to Okra"
Southword Journal: "Death of Alaska"
North Carolina Literary Review: "Water Signs"
The Shoal 2012: "Talking to Okra"
Wisconsin Review, Volume 47, Issue 1: "Arrow Poison"
Heyday Magazine: "Sailing on a Sloop with Strangers, Killaloe to Toomegranny"
fresh literary magazine: "Calving Under the Moon"

Contents

III. Self

I.

Family

They used to pour millet on graves or poppy seeds
To feed the dead who would come disguised as birds.
I put this book here for you, who once lived
So that you should visit us no more.

From *Dedication* by Czeslaw Milosz
translated from the Polish by the author

Death of Alaska

My white German Shepherd,
female ears tuned to sounds
I could not hear, disappeared the day my son left.

She must have heard him going;
he who cut me off like the sharp snip of scissors
against the papery peony stems.

She, my white cavalier, could not keep
me from the way he redrafted our love,
flinging himself, a young man now, into the universe.

For him I canvassed the stars, glossed against a crepe sky.
For her, I tramped through copsewood and brambles —
flashlight a-beam, calling her name.

But no staccato bark and no cantering boy returned,
and I stood alone in the spring cold midnight.

Aw Go Away Now

I

She stretched out on the bed as tall as she could make
herself, lay there for hours, wanted to be a Bean Garda but
had to be five feet six, needed another inch.

She flattened her spine against the cool feather bed, every
vertebra spread open. Solving crime called her, not the
safety of marriage and fourteen pretty babies.

Stretched flat, cool white sheets pulled her closer. She
watched the rain, a soft sun through the window. She was
poised to move from rural Ireland to Phoenix Park.

Valleys in the mattress filled the spaces in her bones. She
stared at cracks along the ceiling, faded blue paint dropped an
occasional flake; she did not give up on the stretch.

II

But she stayed short and grew round. She rocked the
babies. Empty wooden tea chests became playpens for
round, pink faces, crying from dark coils of curls.

Marys, Maraids, Maes, Michaels, growing in height while
she shrank, children, sucking her bones. Tiny fingers tapping
on tea chests to the tunes of siblings, trotting in circles.

III

The last son grew, off to become a veterinarian in the
North. The news of his disappearance, brought by the
Bean Garda, who was tall and straight, sent her fainting.

Lost at sea, he was diving off the coast of Antrim, the
waves angry and flinging. He floated up and down in the
seas, spinning and spinning in the rough waves.

She waited a week, stretched her too-short spine on the
bed, watched the beaded rain, the days, slow drops on
the glass. In her dreams he came to her.

He was found, washed up on the rocks of an isle in
Scotland, her young man, a corpse, salty and bleached,
gathering dulse under cacophonous flocks of gulls.

IV

Aw go away now and again, her short reply as she stretched
his body out on the long table, washed the salt from his
leathery skin, dressed him in a shroud.

She placed the rosary in his hands, lit the candles all
around him, lay the crucifix on his breast while visitors
kissed his cheeks. And she watched and waited.

A Living Will

I remember whiteness, twice-bleached;
tubes, long coils of translucent snakes
distorting lips, hissing air to lungs. I remember
monitors, dissonant bells, tolling heartbeats;
lights, vulgar, graying complexions chalky-white.

My mother says, *How could you want this,*
letting machines keep him alive? He wanted
A Living Will, got too busy.

But the respirator may give him time for his heart to heal.
Time for him to come back to us, I say to no one.

I remember a day in May, my white-haired father found
the fawn on the path to the lake. He carried it
in his arms back to the house, laid it with a whisper
on an old blue quilt. He spread the jaw with quiet hands,
put human lips to the tiny cavity of pinkness, sighed
measured breaths. Aged hands pressed, scarcely a touch,
not to crack young ribs. He breathed again and again,
the fawn, already dead.

What do you remember, Mother, of what he wanted?

The Mother Vine

"Where the Scuppernong perfumes the breeze at night"
NORTH CAROLINA TOAST

*"A scuppernong is a large white muscadine, the state fruit
of North Carolina."*

My three-year-old fingers push
the large grapes, popping sweetness,
juice slides down a small chin.
Mother you didn't know
I slipped out the slightly locked
screen door, opened early this morning.
Now I am playing under vines that drip
grassy green leaves and bronze balls.

Scuppernong often called
mother vine and suscadine, scuplin
suppydine, suppeydime, white grape,
bullets, bullis and bull — no here is a bull,
who often escapes from his pasture.
I can see his white horns as he shuffles along
looking for fruit through the leaves.

He is looking into my place.
I can see through the tendrils
the white soft fur marking
on his face. I want to invite him in,
but he is busy with the grapes.
I want to reach out and touch
the horns pointed and rough.

Then, I see your face, Mother.
Little pieces of your nose and chin show
through the small blocks of the screen window.

There is shock in your eyes.
Come in right now child! Your voice
pulls me away. You shout again,
but you do not come for me.

Water Signs

I crack the hard claw, pick the tender pink, place it on your
      tongue, blush,
while you hold your newborn against your peach breast,
      hands cooing.
Saul sucks soft mouth, pouts petal pink, knows we are in
      the moon sign.

Male crabs seize a sook, soft, shedding – long ribbons of
      sticky sperm explode.
After one year, myriads of tiny zoeas escape, forage on seaweed,
      luxuriant,
caught in the tangled nets of Oyashio, the "parent current."

Crack, the crab whispers, as I fish for the flesh.
Saul sucks the nipple, your tongue smiles for the pink.
Feeding you feeding him, I find myself caught
somewhere between creature and human.

Arrow Poison

Nahuatl anesthetize their victims,
rub arrows across the backs of dendrobates,
ruby, sapphire, neurotoxin jewels
that regurgitate their stomachs
after eating venomous flies and ants.

That I could regurgitate,
turn my guts inside out;
clench with my lips this out-turned organ;
let flecks of poison, clinging to my maw, drop;
reach around with my hands, flake off
your bitterness, crumbs of envenomed words,
sigh, suck in my belly;
memories of you pooling on the ground.

Being Fourteen

His mother was taken abruptly —
in winter when he was fourteen.
Calder's *Circus* puppets, wire, cork
should have danced on strings,
chords, cadences and music.
Chinese fireworks might have exploded —
thunder dragon, a crescendo
of confetti, crimson sparks and flames.
Mt. Vesuvius, humpbacked mountain,
could have erupted cadmium coals.
But there was only the pane of cold glass
and high-banked snow, quiet and white.

The Deaf Dog

For Steven Earl Winters

I press my nose into the warm, dark odor of hound.
Tears roll off the white, brown speckled fur,
oily as unwashed wool. My throat tightens
when dusk and rain blow in. Closing my eyes,
I see my brother, slender, blond boy
gone at twenty-one. You saved the deaf dog
from the hunter who wanted to drown him.
He was not the first. When you were nine,
you fed melons and corn to two striped raccoons.
In your large teenage hands baby finches waited
for your nudge to fly away. Lost squirrels
sucked milk, shiny drops on your finger tips.
The dog wakes and stretches beneath my face.

Missed

It is cold as we walk deep in the woods,
two hours before morning begins. In silence we go,
you ahead. We listen to the music of the forest,
woodpeckers, squirrels in the tall pines, turkeys,
voices rising, a cacophonous crescendo.
A hawk breaks, glides with the currents.
You are taller, six feet, thin, blond, at home here.
I can see the arrows sticking out of the top
of your quiver, grey feathers. We reach the blind,
climb the crude boards you have nailed to
a Loblolly. I pour some coffee from my Thermos,
hands freezing, exposed without gloves. We watch
the trees shed their frost, grasses uncurl.
We wait, and they come, four of them, one buck,
polished antlers blazing, three does. You slowly, slowly,
quietly lift the bow to your cheek, draw the bowstring,
close one eye, look down the sight with the other,
hold your breath, release. The arrow flies one-half inch
over the top of the buck's back.
Four white tails leap through the trees,
and we both know you have perfect aim.

Shampoo

I stand in the shower,
pressed for time,
classes call.
This is your shower
twenty-one-year old son,
your place;
classes call you too.

When it is to your
advantage, I am
your mother.
Most of the time,
I am "Professor who?"

Pressed for time,
covered in water
and slick soap,
I search for shampoo.

Not on any tub ledge,
not in the mesh bag
that holds your razor,
not on the sink,
not on the floor.

I hop out, dripping.
My soapy hands clutch
knobs of cheap cabinets;
open and slam every door.
Where does he keep
the damn shampoo?
Nothing to do but hop
once more into the tub.

Drying my hair with my hands,
I toss my head back and
discover, wedged between
the wall and towel bar, a bottle of
Aussi Citrus: Makes Your Hair So Clean,
one foot and two inches
above my line of vision.

Counterclockwise

swinging
from
the hands

of
the old
wooden

clock,
time
slowly slips

backward
waiting
for

your
sweet
return.

Washing Turnip Greens

The harrow breaks and smoothes
out the surface. Seeds are sown
in sandy soil, roots reach for the dung.
Planted in June, pared away from the sides
of drills, stripes of emerald earth sun.
In cool water I wash each tender leaf,
remove bits of straw, catch a lady bug
as sand sifts to the ivory basin.
Ancient turnips seasoned the juice
made from carrots and spices.
In the seventh century Sappho whispered
to a lover, *My little turnip*.
Now I caress each tiny leaf for the time
when you will taste green.

To An Ex-Husband on His Sixtieth Birthday

I remember the way you
ladled water over me in the tub,
your soapy palms painting long
strokes down my back.

I watched you move your queen,
a delicate glass piece in your hand,
to checkmate, always a nightly game,
you winning, me nothing to lose.

I waited while you drew
thin lines on ceramic figures,
a peasant girl in yellow, a white apron,
geese waiting for fresh oats.

We hammered four pegs,
the symmetry of a tent into the
sandy soil of Cape Hatteras,
I in a home-sewn turquoise bathing suit.

I stitched while you played
"The Entertainer" on our old upright.
Hours into the night your flying
fingers made music I slept to.

Snow piled and whitened the world
for weeks as we shuffled
canasta cards, sipped sweet snow cream.
You loved our newborn son in white.

Divorce – it is all in the word
apart, from, separate, but
if you sever one decade – me –
you would be only fifty today,
a loss indeed.

Still Life

Mothering is terre verte
not quite blue or green. I paint
two perylene peppers,
chives in a viridian vase,
a watercolor wash, sienna,
a still life interrupted.

Here's a hot flash. Mothering
at my age – out of my melancholic
blues. You, foster daughter,
are budding green, twelve, neither
adult nor child.

I paint your adolescent anger,
hot crimson chilies
too warm for this season,
foster you toward the full moon
of womanhood, capture your laughter
on a white enamel palette,
colors swirling in a dance.

Deckles, lovely, ragged edges,
the wet paper buckles, withdraws.
I dip brushes into transparent
raw umber, glaze shades
of roundness, shape a pear.

You watch with cerulean eyes,
count your rosary, fifty aureolin
spheres, glow-in-the-dark beads,
divided by four rounds. I
glimpse your transfiguration,
my rose-madder genuine daughter.

Reflections on a Foster Child

How many women have you called *Mother*?
So easily the word comes to you.
On to another family, you insert yourself
like a comma, an unnecessary clause.

Isn't this new mother another Mary?
Number two loved her kitchen,
wore pink aprons, liked to kiss you
on the forehead. Mary one smelled
of sesame seed, kissed you never.
Now, Mary, number three, you call *Mother*,
place in her hands that rite.
Along with dinner, lamb and mint sauce,
she can serve up some maternal dish.

Wasn't there a Bridgit who took you
to Saint Gobnait's Shrine, praying
for your salvation? Rose was short
and plump, her red hair splendid.
She took in many children; you
disappeared in the voices. Did Eileen teach
you all those Irish songs, "The Galway Races."
At four you sat on Mona's knee, she read
to you in Gaelic, a single candle
to light the words.

Your birth mother you call Susie.
Trapped by her flair to become a mother,
seven children she labored, but none call her Mum.
Who is your mother? Is she the woman who
pressed your uniform, sent you to bath,
calmed your itchy legs at Mass?

Mothers are no mystery to you as you stare at white
mounds of potatoes, glued to a metal spoon,
sputtering toward your plate.

II.

Place

I know it is infinitely painful to leave a place.

From Friedrich Hölderlin, *A Letter*

Calving Under the Moon

Mozart charges the country air. The cow, midnight black,
lies in the corner of a stall, under a single incandescent bulb;
rubbernecking members of the herd press around the byre.

The acrid odor of manure and disinfectant blend with sweet hay.
Up to his elbows in latex, he wets the ropes in a dishpan of water,
taps the jack together. She turns her cumbrous head;

bovine eyes, brown, gaze beneath pleated brows to see him
lean into her syncopated contractions, but no give there.
Are you sure it's a poly? he asks the old Irish farmer.

Kneeling, he pushes his right arm, inside, up to his shoulder.
On her flank his left hand rests, keeping tempo with her breathing.
She bellows against the moon. Shadows of the gate

fall across his back as a white hoof presents; he attaches the rope,
a loop above the fetlock, a half hitch below, but she outplays him.
Swaying, she rises, runs from birth, jack trailing.

Settling her, trying again, he cups the tiny hoof in his hand,
Pulls the calf in an arc, downward, avoiding hip lock,
        tells the farmer,
Lean gently on the jack. Go with her. Stay with me.

In concert the two of them crank when she pushes,
hold the tension when she rests. Blood bursts red streams,
        shooting stars,
the calf slides out wet, a linen-white face.

She swings, licks the birth, enormous pink tongue working.
Stripping the gloves from his dirt-creased hands, he leaves,
whistling *Violin Concerto No. 1*, allegro moderato.

Lady Gregory's Paper Fans

She sits, grey hair, wearing a black dress,
her weary left hand stops to rest.
She gazes at swans flying, great white wings.
Her wrists braceleted, slender fingers ringed,
creases fine paper back and forth into leaves
around a pivot of grosgrain ribbon weaves.
The fan spreads open on her desk, narrow strips.
Poets, dramatists, artists in black ink dip
to sign their names, recollections of her days-
Synge, Shaw, O'Casey, W.B. Yeats.
Nationalists, folklorists gather in the Irish mist.
A literary revival, a Celtic Ireland they insist.
Remembered readings, long evenings ease,
she opens her diary, fanning friends for a breeze.

Mute Swans

Coole Park

The cob dances for a mate, daring dives,
head dips. He builds a nest, decorating
with pebbles, soft moss, wild flowers, and waits
for her desire. She sits on six smooth eggs
as white as her plumage. He feeds her roots,
tubers, knotgrass, red goosefoot. Her orange bill,
edged in black, fluffed, curved neck, stretches for him.
He returns to peck her unfeathered skin
between the eyes. He helps to warm the eggs
in the clutch. Swanlings soon glide, leave ripples
on Coole Turlough. Protecting his cygnets,
he follows close, staving off predators,
until summer, when the only sound
is the vibrant throbbing of great white wings.

Early E-mail

Parke Castle rises off the shores of Lough Gill,
a fortified manor house, steps, a bawn.
Robert Parke watches the horizon, now still,
alone through the dark, he waits for dawn.

A warring Lord threatens to seize the lands.
The pigeons sleep in soft holes in the stone,
briefly waking for warm human hands.
A round open roof, mist fills the dovecote.

Morning, the messenger, a vellum note.
Pigeons stir with flight, fill the fog with coos.
On her way, she sees the great muddy moat.
Into a morning storm, she swiftly flies.

Watching the sun and stars into the night,
she bravely soars over the Lake of Light.

Knocknagullane, Ireland

I first know you, Ireland, when I step barefoot
on the stone floor of my tiny cottage kitchen.
Through a small window I see the Paps billow, purple.

You rise from melting Pleistocene ice sheets and
carboniferous limestone, weathered in deeply fluted
patterns and ravines, rifts that could swallow a man up.

Grey-blue slabs hold back deep green seas,
lines of moss crisscross granite boulders;
veins of lichen shape networks of pinnacles and gullies.

I walk fields, outlined in dry stone, climb hills,
mist boiling around peaks, and pick blue bells
and bog cotton under a wet sun.

Spring lambs, born of Cheviot ewes
and Galway rams, come too early—not wool really,
but cotton tufts – take their place in the landscape.

Potato farmers slog in wellies along narrow roads
lined in yellow gorse. Black and white dogs,
tuned to commands, herd flocks.

Late into the night, singers bend notes,
songs bound to ageless holy chants. The harp is the wind
playing on the dried tendons of a stranded whale's skeleton.

Ballads rise from pints of black Guinness.
Locals set dance to jigs, reels and hornpipes.
I hear the stories, interruptions to the fiddler's tunes.

But only in the dark, rainy midmorning do I really
know you Ireland as I touch the ancient standing stone,
rock built on rock, softened by the sweet smell of tea and rain.

The Parlour

What sound is made when the soul leaves the body?
I hear nothing, see only your fingertips firmly
on his wrist, the rhythmical throbbing, arterial
contractions of the heart, the science of death
a doctor knows so well.

A father brought home to die, he lies on a bed
in the old chestnut parlour, his white,
long-haired cat curled on his stomach.
At eighty-four he is straight, stoic, always a cap
to cover his bald head.

I sit waiting in a faded chair as you feel your father's
final pulse. A soapstone stove warms
the room, and in the corner sits the cherry piano,
a Quaker hymnal, *Worship In Song*, open
to "Blessed Quietness."

The Kitchen

I copied the colors in Monet's kitchen, blue and white
floor tiles; ochre painted chairs sit around
a long rectangular, farmhouse table. Mustard
walls reflect a glow as the sun rises through a row of windows.

The kitchen is quiet at five when I come down
in high wool socks to throw pine logs into the fire.
I hold a hot mug of coffee with mittens, the room
cold enough to leave a skim of ice in the sink.

Monet's pantry now stands empty, but mine
bulges with jars of canned tomatoes, cherries,
bottles of dandelion wine. I will make pots of lentil soup;
the fragrances of garlic, celery, molasses settle in.

Cassatt, Cézanne, Rodin talked long into the night
with Monet about *the impressionists who see light*
as bathing everything with a thousand vibrant
struggling colors, which at a distance establish life.

But the child who joins me by the stove
does not speak of paint and changing light.
He begs me, "Don't cut my hair, please" as I pick lice,
attached to the base of each hair shaft, tiny yellow nits.

The Library

I plan for my death in this room. I will lie
on the cocoa velvet sofa, gazing out of chestnut windows
to see horses slobber clover in the sun. My family
will bring cups of tea; I will slide away here,
where birds slip down the chimney,
land on the soapstone hearth.

But for now I am dusting the cherry secretary.
A tiny bracelet for a four-pound baby,
china beads, four pink, five blue spell out my name.
Brittle yellow roses, dried to brown, lay flattened
by time, stiffened by a florist wire, once,
a splash of color on my father's grave.

Here I lie for hours, legs stretched out, reading
a small leather-bound copy of *The Winter's Tale*.
Bookshelves line the walls of beaded boards
that shrink in winter to leave open gaps,
expand in summer, boards sidling up together.
Bird nests lining the oak mantle, turn to dust.

My Bedroom

Saul, the child,
born on this bed, is five.
I wake each morning
to gaze at the screw
that dots an otherwise
flawless, sky-blue ceiling.

His father cut
blue, red, yellow
lions, tigers, elephants
out of construction paper;
wired them to the screw,
a floating zoo.

The midwife and I
walked with her over the hill
to the pond. She squatted
with each contraction,
her belly spilling
over bent knees.

For a focal point
I gathered armloads
of wine sumac berries,
ironweed, ryegrass, fescue,
Queen Anne's lace,
dried, brittle snapping
in the November seedscape.

She returned to my bed, and
I sat in a rocking chair
on the upstairs porch,
close to the linen-covered
bedroom window, let her
screams swell over me
until I heard his cries.

The mobile moved
on with the child.
For years the dried flowers,
woven into a wreath,
hung on the kitchen
chimney until
the seeds blew away.

The Pond

SUNRISE

Quakers worship in silence by the pond,
gather in chairs to wait for the sun.
Blankets wrapped around cold shoulders,
watchers regard the fog that conceals still waters.
The morning rises with warmth that burns off the mist;
the pond comes alive, louder and louder, a crescendo
of frogs mating on an Easter morning.

MORNING

We plant flowering elm and weeping willow
that will grow to shade picnics. The saplings shoot
toward the sun. The beaver, bronzed, burnished, drags our trees
to construct mud, stone lodges; underwater entrances give
        way to dens.
They leave the trees like spikes around a fort.
My writers' group bends wire cages around new trees,
poetic license against spring visitors, obstinate.

AFTERNOON

In the afternoon I glance from my book to find the top rim
of a pink snorkel as it slowly glides around the perimeter.
The pink stops, and I know my son is delayed
by frogspawn, gelatinous. I curl my knees
to hold the book, bleaching in the sun, read a page,
watch the pink snake skim further around the periphery.
How many pairs of eyes are lost in the grasses at the edge.

EVENING

The sickle mower cuts like giant scissors,
crimps the stems of tall blades of timothy
and fescue. We hurry under the sun, hold off clouds.
A rake shapes windrows, fragrant tunnels.
The sun runs true, and under the heat,
we walk fields, tossing heavy squares.
Fifteen hundred bales, a week of labor, the clouds move in.

DUSK

Dust, sweat, hay cling to our naked bodies
as we dive into the cool pond.
Late summer evening turns to dim light as dragonflies
skim the surface. We float in inner tubes,
watch the stars brighten. In the dark, we step
up on the dock, and wrapped, cold, wet
in an old quilt, we couple to the sounds of crickets.

NIGHT

Late night, campers dip sticks in the bonfires.
Swirling circles of light go round and round.
Their wet skinniness sits on rocks, marshmallow sugar
drips, their tongues darting for melting chocolate.
Children's voices crack the night with song.
In summer, swamping a canoe, childhood passes
beside the pond.

The Garden

Winter still in his lungs,
he spoons soil into
saved egg cartons
and arranges tiny seeds
in each cup of blackness.

In April sprouting shoots stretch
for the sun while they
stand by for hardening off.

He watches and waters
and remembers
Old Flame, heirloom
tomatoes not forgotten.

A late frost in May surprises,
and he grieves at how dreams
can hasten to the ledge.

In the Neighborhood

I woke at five-thirty to flashing lights, red and blue.
Upstairs my husband dozed through the drama.

A fire truck, police cars parked in front of John's house.
Paramedics came and left quickly.

Probably a heart attack I pondered as I
watched dark turn to dawn.

The hearse came, and they wheeled John out,
zippered in a bag, broad white letters blazed on the side.

My husband slept, tired after treating
so many cardiac patients – a long day.

How quietly John flickered away,
only fifteen feet between our houses.

Surely, two sparks so close, negative and
positive, could have found each other in the darkness.

III.

Self

The protected heart that is never exposed to loss,
innocent and secure, cannot know tenderness;
only the won-back heart can ever be satisfied:
free, through all it has given up, to rejoice in its mastery.

From *Dove That Ventured Outside*
by Rainer Maria Rilke

A Master Could Make Flesh of Marble

You purloin my poem, pluck it, reshape it, a sculptor
casting what you observe, even imagine, in three dimensions
like Luca Della Robbia's enameled terra cotta cantoria.

Is *Hermes Carrying the Infant Dionysus* Praxiteles' or perhaps
a fine Hellenistic copy? It is a slab of sinuously relaxed figures,
the possibilities of chiseled stone. A master could make flesh
        of marble.

Not willing to hear my iambic stresses, you carve stanzas
into your reliefs, your own plastic treatment.
My lines are foreshortened, disordered chiastic phrases.

It is not possible to see the whole of Venus de Milo at once.
We walk around it, a series of projective views,
see only the bronze, infer the negative space.

You sense only from your cast, which are not my stories,
hammer lines into misshaped meaning and leave me protesting.
Even so, the light and shade of my words are humbled by your shadow.

Rodmell, February 25-April 18, 1941

You and Leonard in Brighton. You in the lavatory of
Sussex Grill and later Fuller's tea shop heard scraps of
conversation. You wrote journal musings about women
talking in a lavatory: *two common little tarts; the words had a
strong savour of decaying fish.*

But other fragments, Virginia, were they you fretting for
yourself? *A piece of seaweed floats this way, then that way; the
rush of water floating her up and down.* Brave woman, were
you planning, planning your history?

Days before you knew, once again, you were going mad,
you were *living like a moth in a towel, engulfed in a trough of
despair.* Unable to sit still, to talk with friends, to steady
trembling hands, you tried to cool the tempest.

You told yourself to scrub the kitchen floor, rearrange
the books, make butter, beat the carpets, write a review
of Mrs. Thrale's biography. But the voices came over and
over, your hands too cold to hold a pen.

How good of you, Virginia, to leave a letter for Leonard.
To remember all the *possible happiness* he had given. A
March morning, with ice-cold hands, you wrote,
Dearest... it was all due to you.

Beethoven's Appassionata floated through the lodge door.
More clearly now, you wrote about gratitude, guilt —
always the beast at the door until you, dear lady, had the
courage to cut him down.

On the banks of the Ouse, did you carefully choose the
stone, your accomplice or did you, asleep to its leading
role, pick it up, never look to the ground where it lay?

Was it smooth, a piece of limestone and granite?
How large was it? Not a small, light stone but not so heavy.

To pull such a slight one under the muddy surface of the
Ouse. It lay in the pocket of your fur coat that hung upon
your frame like a too-large shroud.

The river running fast and high. Deep, deep into the
waters you slipped. Flowing speed carried you down the
Sussex Ouse at Rodmell near Lewes. You floated toward the
sun but then wedged under the bridge at Southease.

The flow swelled. You were pulled back to the deep green,
muddy depths of the rushing water. Reaching Asheham,
you rose to the light, your coat spread out like the wings of
a diving gull.

Suicide

The incisive possibility hangs
in the air while a beetle casts
shadows across the linen curtain.
We wait for ruby wine in mouth-blown
glasses, round and open, warming by the fire.

We walk the crush of grey shells beneath
the palms of feet. And hear the shrieks
of seagulls shooting for silver slivers.
Sea foam washes over toes
pressing tiny pools in the sand.

On the rocky hills above the ocean
a lone goat chooses its way
from pale blade to pale blade. The wind
pushes the goat back away from
stepping off into the waiting light.

What is it like to love the insane?
Only you can be well-acquainted
with the desperate knowing of almost.

Haircut

Creativity emerges from a little madness. . . .
KAY REDFIELD JAMISON

When I open the top bureau drawer and see you
flaxen, copper, gold flattened curls
lying there in a Ziploc plastic bag,
I tremble, draw back, pinned by many colors.
I want to look away, but I freeze like glaze on an urn.

Cut off in madness, naturally curly you were –
natural, also this tumultuous temperament,
no artificial here, wild uncultivated currents for a brain –
rapid, reckless, hallucinating me. Moods move
up and down like a child's playtime seesaw.

Take your drugs, he says. *If you had cancer,
you'd try to stay alive.*

I would rather have cancer, I say.
*With cancer they smile, hold your hand;
rub your back with jasmine lotion.*
But there I am, not even a wet facecloth to soothe my bald head.

Nice perm, they'd say. Nothing permanent
about my mood. Some say I shaved you off
because I still had some control over you – but not me –
I know I severed you to have one last good time,
one last dance, as they say.

Caretaker of the Crazymakers

You try to sit tight, but I keep slipping away
like a slick fish – moods too oily to make port. You
want to tune me to my main channel.

You are surprised that I cannot recall the weeks
before I knew you. I am muddled, a floating cork,
Madness is a little death, I cry.

You talk about the true self, the
false self, the diva. This makes me angry,
a raging wave. You are caught in my turbulent current.

I ask you to steer me with a breeze
not a blow. We want as little wreckage as possible.
You smile, and I say, *Okay, I will be gentle with you.*

Yo y Mis Pericos

Four parrots
perch,
one on each shoulder,
two in hand.

Against a dark drop
she wears
a white blouse,
pleats
adorn arms
and breasts.

Parrots in slate
gold, green, crimson
turn slightly
to the viewer.

She worships flocks,
believes them,
they can talk a truth.

Feathers tucked
birds content to rest
her arms are wings
hands delicately ready.

No blurs between
art and life, she
paints through the pain –
poised to fly.

La Gioconda

Mona Lisa Gherardini,
why do you cause such a racket,
just another smiling woman?
Women are presumed to smile,
do smile more than men.
A woman's face is her work of fiction,
wrote Oscar Wilde. So what brings
curious millions to your smile, Mona?

Did your husband, Francesco, smile
when a friend commissioned
your portrait by Leonardo?
You were twenty-four when the Master
began to lay the first tempera on the wood.
Four years you sat, thought about your children,
listened to the flute players, played with the cat.
The painter layered glaze on glaze
until he fell in love with his creation.

In his final years Leonardo wrapped
you in his nightdress, tucked you in his suitcase,
traveled to the Chateau D'Amboise.
The Sun King bought you, four thousand
gold crowns, to hang over his bath.
What did he see, lighthearted woman,
to want you there with him, while servant hands
poured fire-warmed water over his back?

The King obsessed with his own image
ignored you; and so you were carted
off by angry crowds to the Louvre.
But another man, a poet of hubris,
settled you on his bedroom wall. Napoleon
lay against his rich pillows at Tuileries Palace
stared into your eyes until Josephine,
jealous, had you moved.

The thief stole you from the Salon Carré,
hid you under his coat, walked out the oak,
fortressed doors, kept you in an old trunk.
Two years later, coming from the darkness,
you were found. Travelling
museum to museum, Italians cried
Madonna, and wept to have you home.

But back in France here you are
with bulletproof, light-controlled days.
Is it that celebrated smile; those eyes
that follow them around the Salle de la Joconde;
the pulse beating at the pit of the throat;
the dark, gauze veil of virtue or is it, Mona,
the lock of hair that falls slightly across the chest
where you play your cards so closely?

The Wisteria Blooms

Spine against the back of the sofa,
feet stretched out, I suddenly hear the
beating of my heart.
Fear splits my breath
and courses to the bone.
How tenuous it all is.
How often things quit, break down.
Just today the toaster stopped
taking that piece of bread
to the red coils, glowing.

I shift in my seat to cut off awareness,
listen to Vivaldi make its way
through invisible waves and pick up
a book of Whitman. I turn on the lamp,
a circle of light blossoms on black letters.
Through the open window I can see
the drops of wisteria, weaving
over the front porch rails. We planted
the vine a decade ago, lost faith,
then one spring day, it exploded lavender.

Daydreaming I drift to a recent visit
to my son's apartment in the city.
Sleeping on a cot, making do,
chill settled in the middle of the night
and I couldn't move. Deep in sleep,
I felt the warmth of a thick blanket, the coolness
of hands. I asked him the next day how he knew
I slept cold during the night?
He said he dreamed it.
We all hang on.

Sailing on a Sloop with Strangers
Killaloe to Toomegranny

And we touched
round, knees and
ropes and backs
wind and rain,
hips and clouds,
cold and salt,
spray and hands.
Not afraid to rub,
to stroke, to pass
the rope, to tend
the till, to settle
the sail, to caress
in such small quarters.
Until, the wind spent
its squall, lulled soft,
and we took our
places, separate.

Whitby With a Friend

She and I in Whitby. She the poet,
I the teacher, poet in heart,
warm to tea and cream, caress Celtic
crosses, descend flight after flight
of stone stairs to the mouth
of the river Esk, a beryl-green
serpent headed to the North Sea.

I, lying on the old bed, cheekbone
cradled in left palm, watch her.
She smoothes silver shoulder-length
hair, tending her beauty in an oval mirror,
pins jewelry to her sage sweater,
monkeys with the jet brooch,
coil of long-dead snail.

We talk about olive, my olive,
her olive sweaters, and chartreuse
dresses, talk about avocado, lime
and citrine. She bought cashmere, silk,
playing her beauty. I bought a farm,
sap green fields stretching far. I wondered
should I have chosen differently.

Harsh winds blow us to the ocean,
white crests capping verdigris waves.
We hike the edge, Saltburn by the Sea,
trudge through cow pastures.
Ancient waters pull us to the precipice,
but we are sucked in the mud-green ooze,
stuck to the earth's surface.

We study fossil remains, ferny leaves
of primitive palms, ammonites, and
artifacts, fill notebooks
with St. Hilde's life, sketch
a Saxon comb of bone. We are
two pilgrims on the road
from Ellerburn to Hackness.

I Grew Up in a Shell Service Station

Bright yellow shells, shaped like giant scallops,
topped red gasoline pumps, waiting for customers.
Father thought it an affordable home
after he dynamited the pumps out of the ground.
Lula, take the children way up the road, he yelled.

He divided the space – my parents' sacrifice,
cold, an iron bed squeaked with every movement –
our room with one bed, three lined the top. I slept
along the bottom, jostled by three pairs of feet;
a third room kept the kitchen and a washbasin.

On Saturdays, we bathed by the fire
in a large tin tub. The girls went first,
mother ladled long strokes down our back;
father scrubbed young boys' ears and necks,
while we minded for our treats, *Cracker Jacks*.

Sunday mornings, father polished saddle oxfords.
Mother turned the crank on the flour bin,
served bone-white biscuits with black molasses.
Father drew the water for the day. Our bucket creaked
on a chain that let the oak vessel into the stone well.

I wore church dresses, thin cotton,
made from left-over floral flour sacks.
We pasted cards, cut out pictures of the prophets
and copied Bible verses for a father,
who divined home as a Shell Service Station.

NOTE:
Early Shell service stations (petrol stations) were shaped like giant scallops.
The St. James's shell had been adopted after the ancestors made the pilgrimage to Santiago de Compostela in Spain.

First Car

I was twelve when father won first prize
for selling the most candy bars in our state.
He bought a green station wagon Rambler
for us to journey east to visit grandmother.

The older children sat in the back
with a chamber pot under mom's seat
and several towels for my throwing up.
Brother squeezed between my parents.

Father never stopped during
the long, boring, crowded rides.
He reached for a pint under his seat.
Only, Mother and I noticed.

We drove through the night
across flat land by black loblolly pines,
smelling mud, rotting fish, peat
from the Waccamaw swamp.
We could smell my father.

Crossing the ocean bridge,
following sandy roads;
the acrid odor of swamp gave way
to the sweet smell of salt.

Tomorrow father would muck for oysters,
dig a pit for hot coals, layer wet burlap sacks,
create steam, shell hinges spreading.

He would open them for us
in a mitten-covered hand, look for tiny gaps,
shuck through the fluted edges,
feed us the tender meat to slurp.

But oysters were for tomorrow. Slipping
down my grandmother's conch-edged drive,
we unloaded the car, but father was always
the one to throw away the empty bottle.

Stretched

Monday was washday. Four galvanized tubs
sat on saw horses. I scrubbed father's work pants.
Dark green, glistening on a washboard,
the cotton, heavy with water, pulled my small hands
back and forth over the ribs.

The dripping pants, one leg at the time
rolled through the wringer. I turned the crank,
water cold to the bone. They fell flat
for the rinse. Plunging the pants up and down,
I watched for suds.

Swinging the arm across, I pressed
the wet clothes flat into the second rinse,
dipped them in starch,
turned the arm for the last time,
the clean smell of laundry wafting.

Laying the clothes on a picnic table, I
tightened them on a metal stretcher;
then to the line with clothes pins peaking
from an apron bag, I clipped.
They hung like a man about to walk across the yard.

All day I washed father's clothes.
In the evening I ironed to slow tunes,
sprinkling water from an old Pepsi bottle.
With chapped hands,
I pushed the heavy iron back and forth.

Finishing my chores, I, the oldest,
Wednesday's child full of responsibility,
was allowed to stay up to read by a flashlight.
The words of *Lorna Doone*
burning bright in the circle of light.

How I Lost My Skirt While Reciting Hiawatha

By the shores of Gitchie Gumee

when I was in third grade reciting Longfellow's poem to
my class in a red skirt my
mother had made

By the shining Big Sea Water

the tiny snaps she attached to the placket, which is all
that held it together, snapped

Stood the wigwam of Nokomis

the skirt slid slowly down, revealing my white thin slip,
which did little to shield the lines of my underpants

The daughter of the moon, Nokomis

I slipped the skirt back up, held the placket with my
right hand while I continued

*…there the wrinkled old Nokomis nursed the little Hiawatha.
rocked him in his linden cradle / bedded soft in moss and rushes.*

the skirt tight in my hand, the class giggled under the
sharp eye of Miss Tilly

*…Stilled his fretful wail by saying, hush, the naked bear will
hear thee*

Ewa-yea, my little owelet

and I didn't miss a word.

Who Is That Woman?

Who is that woman peering back at me
in those copper pots? Hair the color of oysters,
rays of wrinkles, scattering from two eyes, sallow suns;
neck, a swag of drapery folds?

Scrub, rub, rub those copper pots.
Scour grime, griseous green to the glow.

Who is that woman reflected in those copper pots,
scowling back at me? Shrinking, small hands,
sunspots sprinkled over thin blue veins.
Not the beauty I once knew, auburn, knock-out queen.

Scrub, shine that copper. Who can she be?
The more I rub, the clearer she comes to me.

Talking To Okra

from the son's voice

You lived by the book. While others
rose to the sunrise, you woke to a cup
of coffee and the page left off the night
before. Going to bed, never alone, you
shoved the books to the side like a
gratified lover, the dark lines of poets
inching off the pages into your dreams.

Lacy leaves of a Gingko tree, I'll
remember where I put my keys,
gather up the leaves for tea, you said.
You loved language, saved words like
gems, razzuatazz, berry lime sublime;
luachra, bending notes, sliding note
into note. You never hesitated.

You stared, seared people into your vision.
Impressions became words scrawled
on small pages in black ink.
I said, *You're staring again, Mom*.
You said, *Oh, sorry*.

You speared a grape.
It rolled off your glass plate,
past the artichokes, along the open spaces
between the shoes, right up
to a lady's white satin sandal,
your green eyes riveted.

You wrote in your office, overstuffed
armchairs like old men with swollen feet,
papers tumbling out of antique
mahogany chests, a divan covered
in a quilt, dark blocks of mothy wool,
a vase of wild flowers, dried and dusty.

Some would say billions, some millions,
but you saw only one star.
You painted my apartment tomato
and tangerine, listening to books,
cassette player wires trailing from a ragged
blue shirt pocket, covering your heart.
For hours you painted long strokes
of red and orange love for a son.

I have come back to the place where
I left you, here in the cool, dark earth
under the dry stalks, cracked pods
sprouting moist pearls. You created the word.
Out of you came the tomato and orange walls,
the okra, the poem, and me.

Photo: Stephen Arthur Beese

SANDRA ANN WINTERS is an American poet, and frequent visitor to Ireland. She owns a home in Millstreet, County Cork, where she regularly spends time reading and writing. From 1986 to her retirement in 2010, she served as a lecturer of English and Irish literature at Guilford College in Greensboro, NC. She is author of a previous poetry chapbook, *Calving Under the Moon* (Finishing Line Press, 2013).

Her poems have won a variety of awards. "Death of Alaska" won the 2011 Gregory O'Donoghue International Poetry Competition. The editors of the *North Carolina Literary Review* nominated "Water Signs" for the 2011 Pushcart Prize. "Talking to Okra" won first place in the 2012 Carteret Writers 21st Annual Writing Contest. Her poems have been finalists in the 2012 Randall Jarrell Poetry Competition, the 2011 Press 53 Open Poetry Award, the 2010 Rita Dove Poetry Award, and the 2010 Inkwell Journal poetry contest. She received an Honorable Mention in the 2012 Deane Ritch Lomax Poetry Competition.

Sandra Ann Winters' poems have appeared in the *Cork Literary Review*, *Southword*, *the North Carolina Literary Review*, and others.